July Just Doesn't Fit In

By: Brittany C. Carson

Illustrated by: Jerrell Cunningham

Copyright © 2019 by Brittany C. Carson

First Edition 2019

All rights reserved. No part of this book may be reproduced or transmitted in any form or by any means, electronic or mechanical, including photocopying, recording or by any information storage and retrieval system, without written permission from the author, except for the inclusion of brief quotations in a review.

Library of Congress Cataloging-in-Publication Data

Brittany C. Carson

July Just Doesn't Fit In

Edited by: Driadonna Roland

Illustrated by: Jerrell Cunningham

Published by: Brittany C. Carson

Library of Congress Control Number: 2019913829

ISBN: 978-0578576435

10 9 8 7 6 5 4 3 2 1

Printed in the United States of America

Note: This book is intended only as a real life testimony of the life and times of Brittany C. Carson. Readers are advised to consult a professional relationship coach or counselor before making any changes in their love life. The reader assumes all responsibility for the consequences of any actions taken based on the information presented in this book. The information in this book is based on the author's research and experience. Every attempt has been made to ensure that the information is accurate; however, the author cannot accept liability for any errors that may exist. The facts and theories about life are subject to interpretation, and the conclusions and recommendations presented here may not agree with other interpretations.

Cover Design by: NickRichgfx

Visit me at www.BrittanyCCarson.com

July noticed that she stood out from the other kids in her middle school.

She was 12 years old and wore regular clothes — T-shirts, pants, and nice tennis shoes — as did most kids. But she would catch many people's attention by being well put together. Her hair was always fixed up nicely. Her personality was one of a kind. She had a natural glow.

But that did not stop her from trying to fit in with everyone else.

I Am GIFTED and TALENTED

Every day, July would try to fit in with different groups at her school. The first group of students she tried to fit in with were trying to be someone they were not. July was the type of person who would only want to be herself — not copy other students.

She did not fit in the "Trying to Be Someone Else" group. But that did not stop her from trying to fit in with the next group.

I Am
ACCEPTED

The second group July tried to fit in with was always talking loud.

As a person who was quiet and shy, July never wanted to draw attention to herself. She was sensitive to loud sounds. The loud talkers were always noisy so they could be noticed.

She did not fit in the "Loud Talkers" group. But that did not stop her from trying to fit in with the next group.

I Am
ENOUGH

The third group July tried to fit in with was the gossipers. The gossipers would talk about everyone in the school in a bad way.

July was the type of person who minded her own business. She had a big heart, which was filled with lots of love for herself and others. She was humble, and never looked down on the next person.

She did not fit in with the "Gossipers" group. But that did not stop her from trying to fit in with the next group.

I Am
FEARLESS

The fourth group July tried to fit in with was just negative people.

The negative people group was always trying to bring others down. They were angry, sad, and in a bad mood, so they would take it out on other kids.

July was happy most of the time. She kept a positive attitude, spoke nice things, and was in a good mood.

She did not fit in with the "Negative People" group.

I Am
HAPPY

So finally, July got tired of trying to fit in with everyone around her.

July looked at herself in the mirror and decided that she was not meant to fit in with everyone else around her. She was created to stand out.

She saw the glow that was around her, and she started smiling. July told herself that it was okay to be different. She let go of wanting other people to accept her and decided to believe in herself.

Then, she started to embrace who she truly was.

I Am CONFIDENT

A few days after that, July went to school and kept to herself.

She did not try to fit in to groups that were not for her. She was cool with most of the students in her school, but was not interested in hanging with them.

July did not change anything about herself. She just stayed true to herself and stayed out of the other people's way.

I Am
AWESOME

Soon other students started to follow July's lead of being themselves. They started to look up to her.

The glow July carried with her had a positive effect on everyone. She had an influence on other students not only because she was different, but because she embraced it and took her own route.

When she noticed that, July was proud that she chose to just be herself.

I Am KIND

To MYSELF

and OTHERS

It is okay to be different. You do not have to fit in. Just be yourself and let your light shine!

I Am
CREATIVE

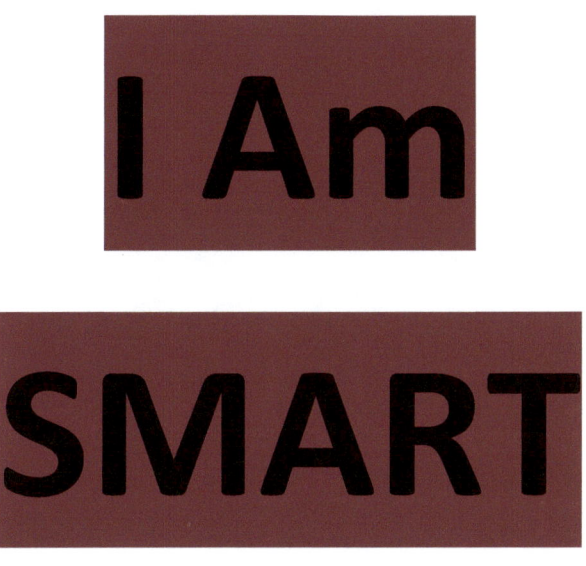

I Am UNIQUE and SPECIAL

I Am CAPABLE of DOING GREAT THINGS

I Am
LOVED

The End

www.ingramcontent.com/pod-product-compliance
Lightning Source LLC
Chambersburg PA
CBHW041813040426
42450CB00001B/29